2

THANK YOU
FOR BEING
A FRIEND

THANK YOU FOR BEING A FRIEND

LIFE — ACCORDING TO THE GOLDEN GIRLS

Emma Lewis

Illustrations by Chantel de Sousa

Smith Street Books

INTRODUCING *the* GOLDEN GIRLS

When its pilot episode first aired on NBC in September 1985, *The Golden Girls* brought an exciting new brand of situation comedy to audiences around the world. Never before had a sitcom been centred around four 'older' women who together formed a household that broke the mold of a traditional TV family. Suddenly, there were four older women talking about S-E-X in prime time, and it was FUNNY.

The Golden Girls was an instant hit, rating through the roof and making household names of Bea Arthur, Rue McClanahan, Betty White and Estelle Getty. Audiences loved the weekly adventures of Dorothy Zbornak, Blanche Devereaux, Rose Nylund and Sophia Petrillo, with millions tuning in every week to enjoy the comedic gold that was so much more than just the sum of its parts. The chemistry between the four leading ladies was evident from day one, and a skilful writing team combined with the formidable talent of four of the funniest women in the business solidified the success of the series, with 180 episodes spanning seven seasons made between 1985 and 1992.

The Golden Girls was not only a well-written comedy, it also raised issues that many other light entertainment programs at the time wouldn't touch. Although mainstream audiences found much of *The Golden Girls* to be familiar and relatable, many episodes courted controversy by covering a litany of topics that were largely taboo for a late-eighties TV audience. Although topics like homosexuality and HIV/AIDS were challenging issues to cover in a thirty-minute prime-time comedy, the writers skilfully wove them into the storyline, informing viewers about topics that many had never been exposed to before.

Fast forward to thirty years later and audiences are still in love with *The Golden Girls*. Seldom out of syndication since its first airing, it remains one of the most adored American sitcoms of all time. Unlike many of its contemporaries, *The Golden Girls* has survived the ageing process and is still relevant to audiences today. More than anything else, it is probably the fantastically dated outfits worn by Blanche and Dorothy that provide a timestamp for *The Golden Girls* world, with this nostalgic nod to late-eighties fashion only adding to the appeal many decades later.

This book has been lovingly written to reflect on one of the greatest TV shows of all time, and to pay homage to four hilarious badass women who changed the face of television comedy forever. It is also dedicated in loving memory of the Golden Girls who are no longer with us, and to my grandparents, who let my sister and I stay up 'late' as children so that we could watch *The Golden Girls* as a family.

So sit back, cut yourself a slice of cheesecake and enjoy revisiting some of television's most beloved characters, the Golden Girls.

The Golden Girls' GOLDEN RULES of FRIENDSHIP

The Golden Girls set the 'gold' standard for great friendship, during the good times and the bad. The following tips will ensure your pals will always thank you for being a friend.

BE HONEST, NOT CRITICAL

If your friend wants to know if her behind looks big in a dress and it looks like she is trying to smuggle a beach ball out of the store, be gentle in your honesty. Simply suggest something else from the rack that will bring out her eyes (and not make her look like she has had her gravitational pull documented by NASA).

BE GREAT IN A CRISIS

This means turning up at any hour with wine, ice cream and any other emergency items required when things go wrong.

LEARN HOW TO KEEP A SECRET

Nobody likes a tattle tale! If your friend confides in you, never ever tell. Not even if the secret is more explosive than a boiling pot of marinara sauce.

NEVER FIGHT OVER A MAN

Men come and go, but a good friend will be yours forever. No man is worth arguing over. Decide by flipping a coin, admitting to yourself that Blanche always gets the best dates and just move on.

BE A GOOD LISTENER

This is not only important for friendships, but is the number one rule for good conversations. Don't just sit there killing time while waiting for your chance to take centre stage. When people do this it is more obvious than Blanche wearing a low-cut blouse at a singles dance.

PAY ATTENTION TO THE DETAILS

When your friend gets home from the salon, be sure to compliment her fantastic new hairstyle. If the haircut makes her look like Willie Nelson after a session of hot yoga, enact the first rule.

Spotlight on
BETTY WHITE

Betty White was born on January 17, 1922, in Illinois, Chicago. Despite wanting to become a forest ranger, White pursued a career in acting after developing an interest in performing at high school – and after she found out that women were not allowed to be forest rangers in 1940! White got her start on radio in the forties, but this was interrupted by World War II, during which she joined the American Women's Voluntary Services. After the war, White worked extensively in radio and television for nearly two decades before her break out, hosting and appearing on dozens of game shows.

While White was an established name on radio and on television, she shot to fame in the seventies as the man-crazy and sharp-witted Sue Ann Nivens in *The Mary Tyler Moore Show*. For this reason, White was originally cast as Blanche in *The Golden Girls*, while Rue McClanahan read for the role of Rose. White and McClanahan decided they weren't happy with the original casting, so they read for each other's roles during screen-testing and the rest is history.

Like her Golden Girl contemporaries, White is an animal-rights activist who is actively involved in many animal-welfare organisations. Perennially popular among viewers young and old, White holds the record for the longest-spanning television career of any woman and is one of television's most beloved stars.

BETTY

WHICH *Golden* GIRL *are* YOU?

Did you know that every human being on Earth can be divided into exactly four categories based on which Golden Girl they most relate to? Well now you know! Reveal your inner Golden Girl by taking the following quiz.

1. **You're at the grocery store and a handsome man catches your eye. To get his attention, you:**
   a. Drop your handkerchief in front of the melons and take the opportunity to show off your bosom while bending over to retrieve it.
   b. Try to strike up a conversation by talking about the delicious melons in St Olaf.
   c. Keep shopping. Why would I approach a stranger at the supermarket?
   d. Take advantage. Have him get something off a high shelf for you.

2. **Your friend is miserable after a messy break-up. The best thing to do is:**
   a. Set her up on a blind date so she can move on quickly.
   b. Invite her over for a crafting session. Everyone is cheered up by crafts, right?
   c. Subtly suggest to her that men are as useful as a sunhat on the surface of Mercury.
   d. Cook her a comforting dinner and watch re-runs of *Miami Vice* together until she falls asleep on the sofa.

3. **Your fashion sense could be best described as:**
   a. Luxurious and low cut.
   b. Almost entirely based on sweater vests.
   c. Big shoulder pads, bigger collars.
   d. Grandma chic.

4. You get distracted after filling your car with gas and drive off without paying. As soon as you realise what you have done, you immediately:

a. Return to the gas station to apologise and flirt outrageously with the attendant. Then start dating him.

b. Return to the gas station, pay for your tank and tip the attendant $20 for wasting his time.

c. Return to the gas station, pay for your tank and then destroy the attendant with a wisecrack that reduces him to tears after he tries to flirt with you.

d. Keep driving, then pretend to not speak English when the cops catch up with you.

5. A close friend asks you to pick them up from the airport but you don't have the time. Your excuse is:

a. I won a beauty contest and I must pick up my prize money immediately.

b. I wouldn't make an excuse! Off to the airport I go.

c. I'd tell them that I've got a flat tyre and then eat half a cheesecake feeling guilty about it.

d. I'm too old to drive. Do you want someone to get killed?

6. Describe your perfect man in a single sentence.

a. Tall, handsome and with a huge wallet.

b. Tall, kind and happy to listen to long stories with no punchlines.

c. Anyone taller than me!

d. Any man who will live long enough to make it to dessert.

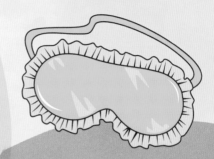

7. **You arrive home to discover a tray of cookies cooling on the window sill. The best thing to do would be:**

   a. Forget about it. This figure didn't happen overnight, sugar!
   b. Leave them be. It would be dishonest to take one.
   c. Eat one.
   d. Eat five, get chest pains, go back for one more.

8. **While dusting, you discover that your roommate has left her journal open on her desk. The best thing to do would be to:**

   a. Ignore it. But if your eyes should casually glance across a page or two of juicy details, so be it.
   b. Ignore it! It would be wrong to take a peek.
   c. Take a passing glance, there could be some good material in there.
   d. Who are you kidding? I'd read the whole thing. Forgive me, I had a stroke!

9. **Your roommate meets a man and you just can't stand him! The best thing to do is:**

   a. Drag her to a singles bar and help her find someone better.
   b. Scare him off by telling a long story about your pet pig Mr Snuffles, who stowed away in a truck to Chicago and eventually tearfully surrendered himself to the Oscar Mayer people.
   c. Reduce him to nothing with a one-liner that will have him running for cover.
   d. Put a Sicilian curse on him.

MOSTLY A'S?
You are a
BLANCHE

You are a sophisticated dame who knows what she wants and how to get it. You love to party and take every opportunity you can to get dressed up and hit the town. You are flirty and outrageous and ooze self-confidence. Your friends love you because you are so much fun.

I'm from the South.
Flirting is part of
my heritage.

MOSTLY B'S?
You are a
ROSE

You are a true optimist with a heart of gold. Always wanting to do the right thing might seem boring to others, but for you it is a way of life. Your beautiful soul makes the world a better place and your friends and family love you for it. Never change!

MOSTLY C'S?
You are a
DOROTHY

You are whip smart, hilarious and fiercely independent. You are a formidable opponent in an argument and you hate to be wrong, but despite your sometimes steely exterior, your actions come from a good place. Your enviable wit and great sense of humour make you very popular.

MOSTLY D'S?
You are a
SOPHIA

You have life experience in spades and you aren't afraid to express your opinions. If somebody messes with you or with someone you love, they had better watch out. However, if you like someone they are in for a treat! Your generosity, wisdom and exceptional cooking skills mean that you will never be lonely.

BLANCHE DEVEREAUX'S GUIDE to SEX & DATING

Are you looking to improve your dating techniques? Want to know how to decide who's worthy of an invitation into your boudoir? You should consult an expert, and there's no greater expert than Blanche Devereaux.

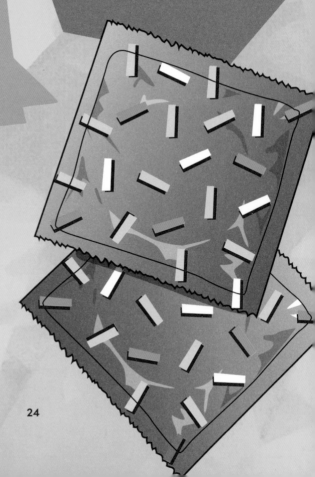

Manners are important

The way he treats you when you first meet is one thing, but you can tell a lot about your date by the way he treats everyone else. If your date is obnoxious and rude to those around him, what makes you think he'll be any nicer to you once the novelty of new romance wears off?

24

Money matters

Nowadays it is no longer expected that the man pays for everything. Always offer to split the cheque. Unless of course he insisted on ordering for you, in which case honey, let him pay and then run for the hills!

Scent is a powerful aphrodisiac

Before I walk out the door I always ensure that I smell sweeter than a Georgia peach. And don't even think of saving your best perfume for special occasions – always treat yourself to a spritz of your favourite scent because EVERY day is a special occasion.

Leave a little something to the imagination

A bit of mystery will leave them begging for more. When it comes to the fabric covering your bosom it's best just to give a little preview … don't spoil the ending! Perfect an air of mystery and you will soon be chasing suitors away with a big old stick like I do.

Chivalry isn't dead!

Even a fierce, independent Southern woman like me likes to have a door held open for her.

The kiss goodnight

You can tell a lot about a man by how he kisses. I have found that the best kissers make the most passionate lovers. A great kisser is somehow gentle and firm at the same time, and will sweep you off your feet while holding you tight.

Be selective about who you invite into the boudoir

Now, a modern woman can take home as many gentleman callers as she likes. However, it pays to be a little selective at the end of the evening or else it will become a full-time job just keeping up with everyone on your dance card. Remember that there is a fine line between having a good time and being a wanton slut. I know. My toe has been on that line.

AND ON TO A
NAVAL
BASE!

Spotlight on RUE McCLANAHAN

Rue McClanahan was born on February 21, 1934, in Healdton, Oklahoma. She studied theatre at the University of Tulsa and made her 1957 stage debut at Erie Playhouse in Pennsylvania, in *Inherit the Wind*. McClanahan began acting in Off-Broadway productions that same year and made her Broadway debut twelve years later playing Sally Weber in the original production of the musical *Jimmy Shine*.

McClanahan's television career began in 1970 after she was cast as Caroline Johnson in *Another World*. Following her popularity in this role, she was cast as Margaret Jardin in *Where the Heart Is*. Like Bea Arthur, McClanahan's breakout hit on television was in the show *Maude*, where she had a six-year tenure in the role of Maude's best friend, Vivian Harmon.

In 1985, McClanahan was cast in *The Golden Girls*, and the legend of Blanche Devereaux was born. She was nominated for four Emmys for the role, winning in 1987 for Outstanding Lead Actress in a Comedy series. Outside of television, McClanahan was an active supporter of gay rights and marriage equality in the United States and was a vegetarian and staunch animal-rights activist.

RUE

The Art of the MIDNIGHT SNACK

Is it late at night and you just can't sleep? Got a hankering for a little something but you can't quite put your finger on what you're craving? Sweet or savoury, hot or cold, nobody does a midnight snack better than the Golden Girls.

Throughout the series, there was a seemingly endless supply of delicious food served up in the Golden Girls' kitchen. Notable late-night favourites included cheesecake, cookies and ice cream – but not everything prepared in the Golden Girls' kitchen after dark sounds so delicious. Less favourable options included Rose's Sperhüven Krispies, a foul-smelling Scandinavian snack, apparently served in St Olaf during 'Viking times'. According to Rose they taste like cheesecake, strawberries and fresh ice cream all at once, you just have to hold your nose when you eat them.

There are no real rules for preparing the perfect midnight snack, but do as the Golden Girls do and always make enough to share, because you should never midnight snack alone!

Did you know that cheesecake was served over one hundred times at the Golden Girls' house? The kitchen table was the command centre for every crisis, and at its centre often lay a delicious cheesecake. From a basic baked cheesecake through to double fudge chocolate, the girls enjoyed a vast array of cheesecake varieties. On page 33 you'll find a fool-proof cheesecake recipe that can then be modified with the variations on pages 34 and 35, to pay tribute to each Golden Girl.

SOPHIA'S MARINARA SAUCE

Marinara sauce was a fixture of the Golden Girls' kitchen, and Sophia Petrillo prided herself on a sauce so delicious it would bring a tear to the eye. The recipe below will be sure to take you back to sunny Sicily with every delicious mouthful.

2 x 400 g (14 oz) best-quality Italian whole peeled tomatoes

125 ml (4 fl oz/½ cup) white wine

60 ml (2 fl oz/¼ cup) olive oil

½ onion, finely diced

4 garlic cloves, finely chopped

½ teaspoon dried oregano

1 teaspoon salt

¼ teaspoon freshly ground black pepper

Pour the tomatoes out into a bowl and swish the wine around in the cans to get all of the juices. Roughly crush the tomatoes using your hands.

Heat the oil in a large cast-iron skillet over medium heat and sauté the onion and garlic for 2 minutes. Add the tomatoes and the wine, along with 125 ml (4 fl oz/½ cup) of water, the oregano and the salt and pepper.

Simmer the sauce for about 10 minutes. Taste and add more oregano and/or seasoning if required. Simmer for a further 5 minutes or until thickened and the oil on the surface is a deep orange.

CLASSIC CHEESECAKE

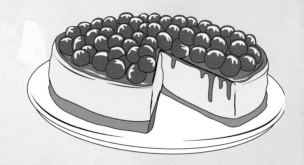

6 tablespoons caster (superfine) sugar
2 tablespoons cornflour
500 g softened cream cheese
2 teaspoons vanilla extract
4 eggs, separated
200 ml (7 fl oz) thickened cream

Base
150 g (5½ oz) graham crackers (digestive biscuits)
75 g (2¾ oz) butter, melted
1½–2 tablespoons caster (superfine) sugar

Heat the oven to 200°C (400°F).

To make the base, crush the biscuits by either whizzing in a food processor or placing them in a plastic bag and giving them a good whacking with a rolling pin. Transfer to a mixing bowl and stir in the melted butter and the sugar. Press over the bottom of a 23 cm (9 in) springform tin and bake in the oven for 10–15 minutes, then remove and leave to cool.

Reduce the oven temperature to 150°C (300°F).

In a large mixing bowl, combine 4 tablespoons of the sugar with the cornflour Add the cream cheese and vanilla and beat with a wooden spoon until smooth. Add the egg yolks and the cream and beat until combined.

Beat the eggwhites to soft peaks. Gradually add the remaining 2 tablespoons of sugar. Using a large metal spoon, gently fold the eggwhite into the cream cheese mixture. Pour the mixture over the biscuit base and bake in the lower half of the oven for 45–60 minutes, or until the topping has just set; the cheesecake should still have a slight wobble. Leave the cheesecake to cool in the tin, then chill in the fridge before carefully unmoulding to serve.

CHEESECAKE VARIATIONS

THE SOUTHERN BELLE

To add some southern charm to your cheesecake, splash a little bourbon into the cheese mixture – a quarter of a cup ought to do it. Then take half a cup of dried apricots, peaches or nectarines and chop into small pieces. Stir the fruit through the cheese mixture and prepare as normal. Just like Blanche, this cheesecake is all about the presentation! To serve, take a ripe peach and slice into thin crescents. Arrange the crescents around the centre of the cheesecake, then place a few fresh cherries in the middle. Voila! You've got yourself a delicious Southern Belle.

THE MINNESOTAN ROSE

Make the cheesecake as directed, but add three teaspoons of rose water to the cheese mix before baking. To create a delicious rose syrup to serve with each slice, place one cup of water and half a cup of sugar in a small saucepan on low heat. Bring to the boil and stir gently for around five minutes until a syrup has formed (don't heat for too long or your syrup will turn into hard toffee!). Remove from the heat and add two tablespoons of lemon juice and two teaspoons of rose water. If you'd like to add a little colour, add a few drops of grenadine or one drop of red food dye. Mix well and allow to cool completely. Garnish the Minnesotan Rose with a handful of white and red rose petals and serve each slice with a little rose syrup.

DOROTHY'S DOUBLE CHOC FUDGE

Any self-respecting New Yorker like Dorothy will tell you that the best cheesecake is made with ricotta cheese. And what kind of a Golden Girl doesn't LOVE chocolate? This cheesecake combines the best of both. Firstly, you will need to alter the crumb base slightly. For a chocolate crumb base, you're going to add a quarter cup of cocoa to the butter before combining with the graham crackers. For the cheese mixture, substitute half the cream cheese with ricotta. Now take 250 g (9 oz) of cooking chocolate and melt in a heatproof bowl over a saucepan of boiling water. Make sure you don't splash any water into the chocolate mix or it will be ruined! Stir this chocolate through the cheese mixture along with a quarter cup of cocoa and prepare as normal. To garnish, mix equal parts cocoa and icing (confectioners') sugar and dust lightly over the cheesecake using a fine sieve.

THE FEISTY ITALIAN

Looking for an Italian twist for your cheesecake that Sophia herself would approve of? This recipe is a take on the Sicilian cheesecake which incorporates the flavour of hazelnuts, citrus and brandy. Firstly, you're going to need to change the base a little. Substitute half a cup of graham crackers for half a cup of hazelnut meal then prepare as normal. To the cheese mixture you're going to add two tablespoons of brandy and half a cup of chopped candied oranges and mix thoroughly. To prepare the garnish, preheat the oven to 180°C/350°F. Spread a sheet of baking paper over a baking tray and spread out half a cup of hazelnuts evenly. Roast for ten minutes but keep your eye on them so they don't burn. Let them cool, then sprinkle the hazelnuts over the cheesecake to garnish. Dust with a little icing (confectioners') sugar just before serving.

Girl, Get Your GROOM ON

So what does it take to get a Golden Girl out of the house and into the world each morning? Follow this step-by-step guide to grooming, Golden Girl style!

LUXURIATE IN A BUBBLE BATH

Treat yourself to a nice long bath as often as you desire - you deserve it. And don't be saving those fancy soaps for a special occasion either! What could be fancier than taking a bath?

NAIL IT

You can tell a lot about a person by looking at their manicure, so keep it classy by maintaining your nails. The fun part is choosing a great colour to complement the rest of your look. Keep chips at bay by investing in a quality top coat.

MOISTURISE!

Every Golden Girl knows the benefit of keeping her skin soft and supple. Use a moisturizing face cream every morning and something a little richer at night to fight those fine lines.

BE SCENT-SATIONAL

Feel all dressed up (even in your birthday suit) by dabbing on a little of your favourite perfume. Find your signature scent for every day, but splash out on something daring for evenings to set the scene for romance.

HAIR FLAIR

Golden Girl hair is all about making the best of what you've been given, using the secret ingredient of VOLUME. Straight, flat hair simply did not exist in the late eighties, so find yourself a good volume-building product and get working! A hair curler or five will build extra volume and help frame your face. Finish It all off with a generous spritz of hairspray and you're ready to face the Miami heat.

JUST BEFORE BED

A Golden Girl never goes to sleep with her make-up on! Wipe away your day with some cleanser and apply your night cream. If you've got time, use a mask treatment once a week to keep your skin at its best, and don't forget those cucumber slices to combat puffy eyes.

I'm not one to blow my own vertubenflugen.

YEAH, OPEN TO **EVERYONE,** DAY OR **NIGHT.**

Put your BEST FACE FORWARD

The Girls have a few simple, Golden rules of make-up for always looking your best.

BASE

Start with a good base so your make-up has something to hold on to. A Golden Girl doesn't have time to reapply throughout the day! To a freshly cleansed face, apply a primer that suits your skin type. Try to choose a primer that contains sunscreen – age may be just a state of mind but keeping those wrinkles at bay is a daily responsibility. Now it's time to sponge on a little foundation and finish with some pressed powder. Voila! Your canvas is ready.

BLUSH

A Golden Girl is never seen without her blush! Blush emphasises the cheekbones and gives a youthful appearance. Choose a nice flattering colour that complements your skin tone – a beautician at your salon can help you choose which blush is best for you. Add some bronzer over your cheekbones and jawline if it's been a while since you've seen the Miami sun.

EYES

Well a little bit of coral never hurt anyone, did it? To perfect the late-eighties eye, you're going to need a coral eyeshadow palette and a heavy hand! Once you've coloured your lids, line your top lashes with a little pencil, then make your eyes pop with two coats of mascara. For a big night out, treat yourself to some glamorous fake lashes.

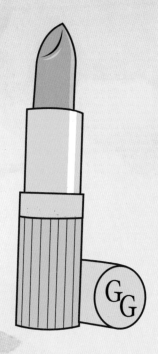

LIPS

Finish your look with the perfect lipstick. Consider the colour of your outfit and your eye make-up – it's usually best to go for a bold eye or a bold lip, not both at once. Don't be afraid of a bold lip if you want to get a little attention, just use a little lip primer to make sure that colour lasts all evening.

The Golden Girls
TOP TEN GREATEST EPISODES

Want to reacquaint yourself with *The Golden Girls* but only have a couple of hours to spare? Here are ten great episodes that are essential viewing for all comedy fans and will most likely convince you to go back and watch the whole series.

'Pilot' (Season 1, episode 1)

A very tight first episode by any standards, this storyline established *The Golden Girls* as an overnight success. In this episode, Blanche becomes engaged and Dorothy and Rose fear they will have to move out of her house when they have only just moved in. We also meet Sophia for the first time, who moves in with the girls after her retirement home burns down following mysterious circumstances.

'Flu Attack' (Season 1, episode 21)

In an era before the concept of 'man flu' existed, four women alone in a house sharing a head cold set the standard for sick and sorry wallowing. The Golden Girls find themselves ill, tired and cranky with each other, culminating in Rose asking if there is any orange juice left, to which Dorothy responds by pouring herself the last of the juice and chugging it as Rose looks on.

'The Way We Met' (Season 1, episode 25)

'The Way We Met' is the perfect end to the fantastic first season of *The Golden Girls*. In this episode, we are transported to the past to finally find out how the Golden Girls' household first came to be. The highlight of this episode is the flashback to when the girls go to the grocery store together for the first time and squabble over the contents of their cart.

'Ladies of the Evening' (Season 2, episode 2)

In this hilarious episode, Blanche, Dorothy and Rose are arrested on the way to a movie premiere after being mistaken for prostitutes. The girls end up behind bars before Sophia arrives under the guise of bailing them out, only to take the tickets to the premiere for herself. When one of the local call-girls attempts to start a fight with Blanche in jail, Dorothy steps up to defend her friend and hilarity ensues.

'Isn't It Romantic?' (Season 2, episode 5)

'Isn't It Romantic?' sees Dorothy's friend Jean visit from out of town. After striking up a friendship with the other girls, Jean lets her romantic feelings towards Rose be known. *The Golden Girls* was one of the first prime-time sitcoms to feature a lesbian storyline. In 1987 this episode was nominated for the Emmy for Outstanding Writing for a Comedy Series and won the Emmy for Outstanding Directing for a Comedy Series.

'One for the Money'
(Season 3, episode 2)

Picture this: Brooklyn, 1954. This is a flashback episode where the girls reminisce about their many attempts to earn extra money. In a flashback to the 1950s, a young Dorothy goes to visit Sophia, asking her mother to watch the children so she can take on extra work to save for their first television set. In this scene, Estelle Getty appears without ageing make-up as her 'younger' self. Also, watch out for the comedy gold when Blanche, Dorothy and Rose take part in a dance competition.

'Valentine's Day'
(Season 4, episode 15)

Another flashback episode but with all new material, this episode sees each of the girls stood up by their dates on Valentine's Day. Essentially a highlights reel of Valentine's Days past for each Golden Girl, this episode contains the famous scene where the girls go to buy condoms before travelling to the Bahamas.

'72 Hours' (Season 5, episode 19)

The Golden Girls never shied away from a sensitive topic, and in 1990, there was no more sensitive topic than HIV/AIDS. It turns out that Rose had a blood transfusion five years earlier during a gall bladder removal and is called back to the hospital after it is revealed that a possible contamination has occurred. Of course, it all works out in the end, but this episode helped to dispel some of the common myths going around about HIV transmission at the time.

'Sister of the Bride' (Season 6, episode 14)

Another great episode of *The Golden Girls* that deals with attitudes towards homosexuality, 'Sister of the Bride' sees Blanche's gay brother Clayton visit Miami to wed his partner, Doug, in a commitment ceremony. At first Blanche is worried about her brother because of what others might think, but in the end, she is totally accepting of their union. The scene where Dorothy must physically restrain Sophia from reacting when Clayton suggests that Doug would 'bend over backwards' for him steals the show.

'One Flew Out of the Cuckoo's Nest' (Season 7, episode 23)

This is the series finale that sees Dorothy marrying Blanche's uncle Lucas. What begins as a practical joke Dorothy and Lucas play on Blanche after she sets them up on a blind date, soon blossoms into a whirlwind romance. Dorothy accepts Lucas's proposal and leaves the Golden Girls' house after a tearful goodbye, setting the scene for *The Golden Girls* spin-off *Golden Palace*. This is a touching and hilarious episode that even sees Stan and Dorothy finally make peace, with Stan posing as Dorothy's limo driver and giving her his blessing on the way to the ceremony. Get those tissues ready for an emotional goodbye!

Ask the GOLDEN GIRLS

Dear GG,

I have been happily married for ten years, but recently my husband has been coming home late from work and is suddenly taking weekend work trips. I also found new underwear in his drawer! Is he seeing someone else? What should I do?

— Scared

Got a problem? The Girls have got your back.

I'll handle this, ladies. You should trust your instincts. I remember when Stanley first started cheating on me with that two-bit hussy from the airline. I became slightly suspicious when he started smelling like a man who had just soaked in a bathtub full of cheap cologne. I then became VERY suspicious when he asked me to get his best toupee steam-cleaned. I think you need to confront your husband as soon as possible. If he is cheating on you, dump him like a hot tamale and move on with your life.

46

Dear GG,

My husband died eight years ago, and since then I haven't been interested in dating. Finally, I've met someone who I feel a connection with. Problem is, he wants to go away for the weekend and I am terrified. What if I've forgotten what to do in the bedroom?

- Hesitant

Honey, sex is like riding a bike – you never forget how to do it. And if you fall off, heck – just jump right back on the horse (or so to speak). You just need to relax and let your man make you feel like the only woman in the room. If you can't relax, a glass of French Champagne for courage never hurt anybody, just don't finish the whole bottle at once or your night might be over faster than you think!

It took me a long time after Charlie died to pluck up the courage to start dating again. It was over five years before I spent an evening with another man. My advice is to make sure that you choose a man that you trust and remember what my mother used to tell me, 'The older you get, the better you get ... unless you are a banana.'

47

Dear GG,

From the outside, it appears everything is going wonderfully in my life. I have a great career, I paid for my own home and I have an active social life. The only thing missing is a man to call my own. What can I do to make the final piece of the puzzle fall into place?

– Lonely

Dorothy: Are you kidding? You don't need a man. You have everything that anyone could ever want, except for maybe a lifetime supply of double-fudge ice cream. Enjoy the freedom of living your best life your way.

Sophia: Picture this: Sicily, 1933. A beautiful young woman finds herself with all the trappings of a wonderful life. She is a great beauty, has a home overlooking the ocean and owns a prize-winning dairy cow that never dries up. She, too, longs for what you long for – a husband to share it all with. Well, let me tell you, one day she did meet a man, and they got married in front of that house overlooking the ocean. One week later he was dead – kicked in the head by the very same prize-winning cow. Turns out the cow didn't like to share.

48

Dear GG,

I am 35 years old and I'm terrified by the ageing process. Every day I seem to notice a new flaw on my face or body. I just can't stand the idea of getting old! Am I going crazy?

– Concerned

Sophia: Yes. You are going crazy.

Blanche: Oh, sweetheart I know just how you feel, as a woman in her late forties (ahem) I face these thoughts from time to time. Luckily for me I have been blessed with a petite figure and a gravity-defying bosom that seems impervious to the ageing process. I must say, I am a freak of nature in that respect. Also, my skin is still tauter than a snare drum at a county fair on a winter's day. And as for my hair ... well ... I'm sorry – could you repeat the question?

Dorothy: I feel so bad for you. Try to cling to the remaining 45 years of your life with whatever strength you have left. Now pardon me while I go take my hormone replacement pills and stretch out my hump.

Rose: They have a saying back in St Olaf that goes, 'You can put lipstick on the oldest mackerel in the barrel, but you can't make it taste like a perch.' I keep this in my mind when I get worried about getting old and it always makes me feel better.

49

Spotlight on
BEA ARTHUR

Bea Arthur was born on May 13, 1922, in Brooklyn, New York. A love of the dramatic arts led her to study at the Dramatic Workshop of The New School and join an Off-Broadway theatre group at the Cherry Lane Theatre. Arthur spent much of the fifties and sixties starring in Broadway and Off-Broadway plays.

Her TV acting debut came relatively late in her career – in 1971, Arthur was nearly fifty when she appeared on *All in the Family* as outspoken liberal feminist Maude Finlay. The character was so popular that Arthur was offered her own series, *Maude*, in 1972. *Maude* was a ground-breaking sitcom that dealt with highly controversial issues at the time, including abortion, drugs and domestic violence. Maude ran for six seasons between 1972 and 1978, catapulting Arthur to television stardom in the United States. Her comedic timing and formidable wit saw Arthur perfectly cast as Dorothy in *The Golden Girls*, where her hilarious one-liners often stole the show.

Outside of Hollywood, Arthur was an animal-rights activist and gay-rights campaigner. And if you had any doubt that Bea Arthur wasn't totally badass, she also worked as a truck driver in the United States Marine Corps Women's Reserve during World War II.

BEA

Dorothy's guide to
THE WITTY ZINGER

Dorothy Zbornak was famous for her hilarious and cutting one-liners – nobody was safe! Here is some expert advice on dropping a witty zinger just like a Golden Girl.

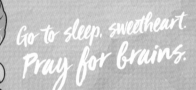

Go to sleep, sweetheart. Pray for brains.

ALWAYS BE PREPARED

There's nothing worse than thinking of the perfect comeback for something said at breakfast while you're lying in bed at night. To combat this, I like to keep a repertoire of zingers at hand so I am always ready. I often come up with them while pretending to listen to one of Rose's stories about St Olaf.

TIMING IS EVERYTHING

There's no point hatching a witty retort ten seconds too late. Which leads me to my next point ...

SOMETIMES NO RESPONSE IS BEST

Knowing when to leave a little 'dead air' before responding is an art unto itself. This silence is best combined with a sardonic glance.

BRING YOUR GAME FACE

Your expression goes a long way when delivering a cutting one-liner. Your delivery should always be deadpan, all of the time. An eyebrow should be the only thing raised on your face – no smiling!

SARCASM IS YOUR FRIEND

Whoever said that sarcasm is the lowest form of wit has obviously never met me. In fact, people who don't think sarcasm is smart probably think that Halle Berry is the latest flavour of ice cream. See what I did there?

WATCH YOUR LANGUAGE!

I don't have a problem with swearing *per se*, but use your curse words sparingly. It's hard to drop a cutting zinger if you sound like a sailor who just dropped an anchor on his foot.

DON'T FORGET THE ONE-LINER

Some people think that the one-liner is dated, but they probably also think that telling a 'knock knock' joke is funny, so what do they know? The best gags require no set-up and are all punchline.

DON'T BE CRUEL

This is a pro tip for those who wish to remain popular. The best zingers are smart, funny and delivered with impeccable timing – they are never nasty or mean-spirited. Be remembered for being hilarious, not for being heartless.

GOLDEN GIRLS SPIN-OFFS

The Golden Girls was hugely popular, so inevitably there were several attempts to replicate its success in the form of spin-offs and companion shows.

While most spin-offs are based around already-established, popular characters, in the case of *The Golden Girls*, new characters were introduced in order to launch Empty Nest. The final episode of the second series of *The Golden Girls* is essentially the *Empty Nest* pilot, in which we meet Dr Harry Weston – a paediatrician who has become an 'empty nester' after the recent death of his wife. Harry is introduced as a neighbour of the Girls, and turns up sporadically for the rest of the series, a favour returned by the cast of *The Golden Girls*, who occasionally pop up in episodes of *Empty Nest*.

Empty Nest was very popular with viewers, and, like *The Golden Girls*, it ran for seven seasons during the late eighties and early nineties. *Empty Nest* even had a spin-off of its own, the relatively short-lived *Nurses*, a series that centred around the lives of a group of nurses working at the hospital with Harry. *Nurses* lasted for three seasons between 1991 and 1994, resulting in a brief period where three programs that shared the same producer and that existed in the same sitcom universe had intermingled storylines. The shows even originally aired on the same night of the week!

Of course, spin-offs can also be the continuation of a series under a slightly different guise – enter *Golden Palace*. At the end of *The Golden Girls*, we see Blanche, Sophia and Rose say goodbye to Dorothy and take over the running of a flailing Miami hotel. Most of the previous staff have left, leaving the Girls to take on many of the jobs around the hotel to make ends meet. *Golden Palace* only lasted a single season due to poor ratings, with the finale seeing Sophia finally move back to Shady Pines retirement home.

If you want my advice, I think you should sleep with him.

Fun fact

Cheech Marin (from comedy duo Cheech and Chong) starred as the hotel's chef on *Golden Palace*, a role originally intended for English comedian Alexei Sayle.

THE 10 Commandments for SHAREHOUSE LIVING

Looking to keep the peace with your roommates? Look no further than these handy tips that always kept the peace in the Golden Girls' house.

1

Thou shalt not eat the last cookie.

Always offer the last cookie to your roommate first, and never eat the last slice of cheesecake ... unless you can guarantee that everyone else is asleep and you definitely won't get caught.

2

Thou shalt not leave dirty dishes lying around the kitchen.

This is a one-way ticket to roommate warfare. Even worse is leaving the basin full of dirty dishes soaking in cold dirty water. Just don't do it!

3

Thou shalt keep loud phone calls to a minimum.

Nobody is interested in hearing your hour-long discussion with Aunt Phyllis about her botched hysterectomy. Keep your voice down if you're on the phone in a common area, or take the call in your room.

4

Honour thy roommate's quiet time.

We all love to have a good conversation, but don't bombard your roommate with chatter the minute they arrive home. At least let your roommate pour herself a stiff drink before you bombard her with the details of your juicy gossip.

5

Thou shalt not commit the sin of interrupting.

If your roommate is telling a story, give her your full attention, and never butt in! Nobody likes to be interrupted, particularly with a story that you think is better than hers. Keep a lid on it, ladies.

6

Thou shalt not covet thy roommate's date.

Even if it's Saturday night and you are alone again, watching *Magnum PI* and eating bonbons on the couch, do not flirt with your roommate's date when he comes to the door.

7

Thou shalt not bore your housemate with what happens in your dreams.

You may have married Don Johnson after your spaceship crashed into the roof of Caesar's Palace last night, but nobody cares!

8

Remember to keep holy the time when your favourite programs are on.

Don't start vacuuming the lounge room just as the opening credits of *Miami Vice* begin. This is sacred time!

9

Thou shalt not spend an hour in the bathroom on a Saturday night.

There is nothing worse than being late for your date because you had to wait for your housemate to finish her long bath. Even worse is being greeted by fogged up mirrors and wet towels on the floor. Keep it short during date-night peak hour.

10

Thou shalt not change the TV channel if a handsome man is on the screen.

Self-explanatory really – if you can already see Tom Selleck, there is nothing else worth watching.

Sophia Petrillo's Guide to LIVING YOUR BEST LIFE

Aside from the fact that I've only ever made love in the one position, I've led a very full life. Here are my tips to living your best life at any age.

HAVE THE RIGHT ATTITUDE

Age is just a number! Sure, sometimes I wake up and feel as if a Mariachi band has been performing on top of my sleeping body for several hours. But life is what you make of it. Forget your age and take life by the horns.

TRY SOMETHING NEW

Variety is the spice of life. I was eighty years old before I lit that fire at the old folks' home, and my only regret is that I didn't do it sooner!

USE IT OR LOSE IT!

Keep your body and your mind active and you'll never feel (too) old. I like to keep active by taking long walks, and I keep my wits about me by playing poker at the old folks' home and robbing those old cronies blind.

KEEP GOOD COMPANY

I might make fun of them all, but without my pussycat Dorothy, that cheap floozy Blanche and that gullible pinhead Rose, life would be very boring indeed.

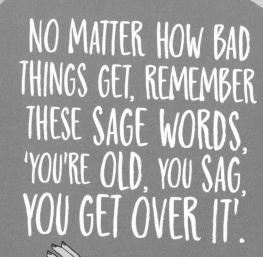

NO MATTER HOW BAD THINGS GET, REMEMBER THESE SAGE WORDS, 'YOU'RE OLD, YOU SAG, YOU GET OVER IT'.

I'M READY! TAKE ME HURRICANE!

IF YOU WANT SOMETHING, GO MAKE IT HAPPEN

This could be your last week on Earth (or last day on Earth if you've just eaten Blanche's cooking). Don't procrastinate or you will end up paralysed with indecision.

Spotlight on
ESTELLE GETTY

Born on July 25, 1923, Getty began her career as a comedian and actor with the Yiddish Theatre in New York City. A love of Vaudeville drew her to the stage where she tread the boards Off-Broadway and in community theatres while working a day job as a secretary. Her most notable theatre role was in Harvey Fierstein's *Torch Song Trilogy* during its original Broadway run in 1982.

After making a name for herself on the stage, Getty went on to have a twenty-year career in television, with roles in shows including *Empty Nest*, *Fantasy Island*, *Cagney and Lacey*, *Blossom* and *Mad About You*. Getty was also a film actor, with roles in *Tootsie*, *Mannequin*, *Mask* and *Stop! Or My Mom Will Shoot*.

The role of Sophia Petrillo was a huge break for Getty who had only had minor roles previously. Her son quoted her as saying at the time, 'After fifty years in the business, I'm an overnight success.' Despite playing the role of an octogenarian, Estelle Getty was the second youngest of *The Golden Girls* cast, spending forty-five minutes in the make-up chair before each episode to look the part.

Between 1986 and 1993, Getty was nominated for seven Emmy awards for Outstanding Supporting Actress in a Comedy Series for *The Golden Girls*, taking out the award in 1988.

ESTELLE

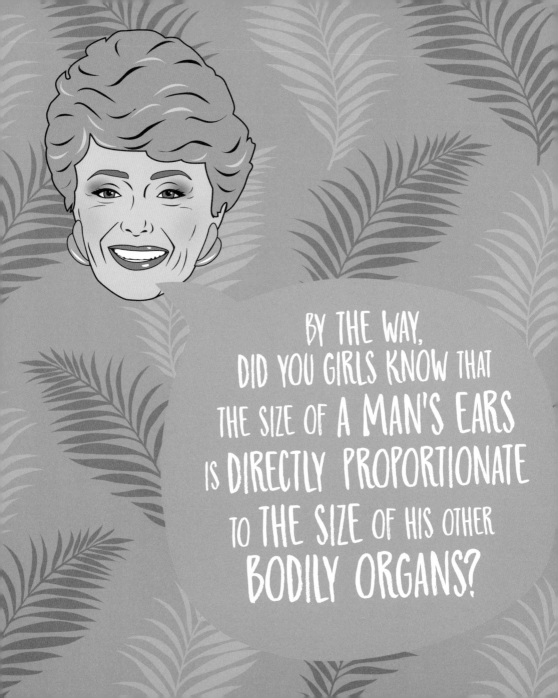

The Golden Girls' definitive guide to
FABULOUS FASHION

Fashion may be fickle and styles will come and go, but the outfits on *The Golden Girls* will endure through the ages. Watching an episode of the show today is like peering into a perfectly preserved time capsule of late-eighties and early-nineties women's fashion. The costumes in *The Golden Girls* may appear a little outrageous compared to today's fashions, but remember that in 1985 it was perfectly acceptable to get around in eye-searingly clashing patterns and bright, shiny fabrics so synthetic they could start a small forest fire with static electricity.

The glamour of Blanche Devereaux's seemingly infinite wardrobe is as memorable as Dorothy's inexplicable array of large-collared long-sleeved garments. But what was most notable was that for the first time on network television, older women were stepping out in fashion-forward clothing, sending a clear message to the world that style does not end with youth.

The hard work that went into wardrobe for each episode did not go unnoticed – *The Golden Girls* costume designer Judy Evans was nominated for an Emmy in 1985 for Outstanding Costume Design for a Series but lost out to the costume designer for *Murder She Wrote* (Angela Lansbury sure could work a pantsuit). The universe corrected itself four years later when Evans won the same award for her work on the short-lived sitcom *Beauty and the Beast*, a fantasy drama centred on the romance between an LA district attorney and a kindly lion-man, written and produced by none other than George R. R. Martin of *Game of Thrones* fame.

So you want to dress like a Golden Girl? The following pages have everything you need to emulate the iconic looks of Blanche, Dorothy, Rose and Sophia.

GET *the* LOOK

Looking to make your wardrobe a little more Golden? With just a few key pieces, you'll fit right in on the lanai.

A figure-hugging LBD with a low neckline and shoulder pads is indispensable. Team this dress with some cute heels and you are ready to hit the town!

Black dress

Robe

In silk or satin, for swanning about the house.

Keep them on a chain around your neck so you never lose track of them.

Glasses

Think styles that draw the eye. Big bright and chunky for day wear and sparkles for the evening.

Earrings

A long necklace is a key accessory – the longer, brighter and chunkier the better.

long necklace

Invest in a bold, long jacket, replete with a confusing array of colours and textures. Don't forget the shoulder pads.

Jacket

Scarf

Add a little flair to your look with a jaunty scarf in a colour that complements the rest of your outfit (or a pattern that clashes).

Sweater

Look no further than to Rose for sweater inspo. Choose a pastel colour, preferably decorated with folksy embroidery.

Heels

Age is no barrier to footwear if you're a Golden Girl! Go metallic for a little extra glam.

Fashion profile
BLANCHE

There's no denying it – Blanche Devereaux is a style icon. Blanche's outfits were as bold and brash as the sexy southerner herself. Audiences loved seeing her stylish and often outrageous outfits. From day through evening, Blanche epitomised glamour and oozed confidence.

Want to dress more like Blanche? Think bright colours and bold synthetic fabrics. A dress should always be tight enough to show off your curves, with a neckline that plunges just enough to reveal an ample bosom. Accessorise with heels as high as you can muster and a cute purse. Never be seen without earrings!

Of course, for Blanche, dressing to impress doesn't end when she gets home at night. It's no surprise that one of Blanche's key looks is her nightwear. Blanche's sexy sleepwear is defined by the luxurious satin robe. Reportedly, Rue McClanahan loved her on-screen sleepwear so much she kept it all after shooting. Team your floaty gown with a sexy slip and you will be boudoir ready.

Plunging
neckline

Luxe
accessories

Cinched
waist

Bright bold
colours

Sassy heels

Fashion profile
DOROTHY

Did somebody say BIG collars? Dorothy's incredible wardrobe consisted of styles that were modern and fashion-forward, and notably provided some much-appreciated style inspiration to a generation of tall women.

To dress like Dorothy, think layers, layers and more layers. Dorothy often wore long tops and structured jackets that enhanced the taller figure. Team a neutral-coloured high-neck blouse with a tailored long jacket in a contrasting colour. Dorothy liked to mix patterns and textures so don't be afraid to experiment. Finish the look with a knee-length skirt and flat boots.

For evening wear, Dorothy loved a long gown with shoulder pads, and she was not shy about a sequin or two. Bold, big jewellery was a key accessory for Dorothy, including long necklaces, chunky brooches and big earrings.

High neckline

Geometric prints

long-line jacket

Statement jewelery

Stylish flats

Fashion profile
ROSE

A slave to the sweater vest, Rose's style is defined by practical outfits with a fun twist. A sweater vest with a cute design teamed with sensible slacks were the order of daytime wear – think the sweater vest with an illustrated farm scene she wore early in the series. Rose loved a tailored pantsuit in a block colour and looked as good in pastels as she did in bolder shades.

Rose's evening look was always classy, flattering and showed a little bit of flair when required. Look to matching top and skirt ensembles for evening wear, ideally with a V-shaped neckline to flatter a rather ample bosom without giving too much away.

Rose was a great dancer and had a killer set of pins to show for it. Her evening wear certainly showed off plenty of her best assets, always complemented with a flattering pair of tights and some heels (or tap shoes when required).

Pearls

Pastel colours

Feminine silhouette

Floral prints

Classic heels

Fashion profile
SOPHIA

Sophia perfected grandma chic with a range of looks befitting a woman in her eighties living in the eighties. Never one to show much skin, high necks and slacks were key to her look, teamed with a sensible pair of flat shoes. Sophia loved a frilly collar and always buttoned to the top.

For evening wear, Sophia chose outfits that were modest but still glamorous – think pantsuits and long skirts. Like all good Italian women of her era, Sophia kept a go-to version of her favourite outfits in black for times of grief.

Sophia's accessories were simple and often functional – her trademark glasses could always be found on a chain around her neck. Sophia's love of cooking meant rocking a multitude of aprons over the course of the show. And who could forget THAT purse? Sophia's purse was never out of her sight – such was Sophia's love for it that she often carried it from room to room in the house.

Cameo brooch

Peter Pan collar

Ubiquitous purse

Practical cardigan

Sensible shoes

Rose Nylund's down-home guide to SMALL-TOWN LIVING

When Sophia wasn't reminiscing about Sicily in the 1920s, Rose was waxing sentimental about St Olaf, the Minnesotan town where she was born and raised. While Rose may have been voted 'most likely to get stuck in a tuba' in high school, the following pearls of wisdom from her St Olaf days will prepare you for any challenges small-town life might throw at you.

FAMILY COMES FIRST

Back in St Olaf, my cousin Joe always used to say that 'you can't raise a barn without a family'. I mean, he wasn't actually much of a family man since he never had any children and he didn't care for family gatherings – I think he just said it so we felt guilty about not helping him move his barn that time. He ended up doing it himself and broke both his legs when a bale of hay fell on him. Regardless, your family is everything. Be kind to each other or you might end up like poor Cousin Joe.

TRY TO FIND FULFILLING WORK

Sure, we'd all love to spend our time whittling cheddar, entering yodelling competitions or staring into the big black hole at the edge of town – but not every day can be a Mardi Gras. At some stage you're going to have to put down your whittling knife and make a career for yourself. It can be hard to find fulfilling work in a small town – as much as everyone would like a go on the butter churn, it's just not going to happen. The best jobs are those you enjoy so much that they don't feel like work at all – like that time I worked the mackerel petting booth at the St Olaf county fair.

YOU CAN LEAD A MULE TO BEAVER FALLS BUT YOU CAN'T MAKE IT ROLL A CHEESE DOWN THE MAIN STREET

In a small town, the locals have probably been around a long time and aren't going anywhere fast (especially old one-legged Sam). In every small town there are going to be people you would rather avoid, but the nature of a close-knit community often makes this impossible. My best advice is to always be kind and patient with everyone. Failing that, dig a deep moat around your house like my uncle Lars did.

MAKE THE BEST OF WHAT YOU'VE GOT

There's no point getting jealous of your neighbour's shiny new harvester. You can hope and pray as much as you like, but it's just going to be you and your old banged-up jalopy until you sell enough turnip extract to pay for a new one. Hold yourself together and remember that the fish paste is always smoother on the other side of the fence.

'I remember, back in St Olaf...'

Who is STAN ZBORNAK?

Let's talk about Dorothy's ex-husband. Stan was a fan favourite, someone Dorothy once described as a 'pig in a cheap suit'.

Stan was played by Herb Edelman, a career film and television actor who before *The Golden Girls* had established himself as a popular recurring guest star on the hit medical drama *St Elsewhere*. Edelman was one of *The Golden Girls'* most beloved guest cast members, with his performance receiving two Emmy nominations for Outstanding Guest Performer in a Comedy Series.

The only reason Dorothy ever agreed to date Stan in the first place was because he claimed to be leaving for Korea soon and she thought he 'would probably die'. Stan and Dorothy got married as teenagers after a one-night stand in the back of Stan's Chevy resulted in an unplanned pregnancy. Stan proposed to Dorothy by planting the ring in a glass of Champagne. Unfortunately, Dorothy accidentally swallowed the ring, which 'turned up' three days later.

Stan and Dorothy's disappointing sex life was a regular topic of jokes throughout the series, with Dorothy suggesting that they conceived their first child in a love-making session that lasted 'about three seconds'. Stan and Dorothy were married for 38 years before Stan began an affair with Chrissy, an airline stewadess nearly 30 years his junior. After their divorce, Dorothy moved to Miami, and despite their separation, Stan continued to interrupt Dorothy's life.

Despite their differences, Dorothy briefly considered a reconciliation with Stan after he turned up on her doorstep claiming it was over with Chrissy. It was not meant to be, but Stan continued as a recurring character throughout the series, all the way through to the final episode.

Hi, its me, Stan!

Sophia & Dorothy on
MOTHER–DAUGHTER COHABITATION

So you've decided to move in with family and need some advice. The good news is that you are not alone! Let Dorothy and Sophia guide you through the often-rocky terrain of mother–daughter cohabitation.

Sophia

Get separate bedrooms. This isn't an episode of *The Waltons*.

Dorothy

Try not to be too critical of each other. Commenting on every little aspect of each other's lives will wear pretty thin after a while – save your opinion for when it really matters, like the time I had to stop Ma from leaving the house wearing a pair of dark sunglasses that made her look like Roy Orbison.

Sophia

Try not to meddle too much in each other's business, unless of course one of you starts dating. This is the ultimate opportunity to scrutinise every minuscule detail of your daughter's life until you can't stand being in the same room together.

Dorothy

Patience is a virtue. Living in the same house will expose you to each other's annoying little habits. Personally, the sound of Ma slurping a bowl of soup drives me up the wall. I find avoidance is key – it's better to take yourself out of the situation than risk World War III erupting over a bowl of matzo balls.

Sophia

Find a hobby you both enjoy, like gin rummy. Then get so good you destroy your daughter every time you play for the next thirty years. You will never be bored because she'll just keep coming back for more.

Dorothy

Try not to sweat the small stuff. If you're lucky enough to be family AND friends, you should take advantage of the quality time you get to spend together. For the not-so-quality time, get earplugs.

MA, WHAT WERE YOU DOING IN MY PURSE?

STEALING!

How well do YOU KNOW the GOLDEN GIRLS?

So you've seen your share of episodes and you consider yourself a huge fan of *The Golden Girls*. But how much do you really know? Test yourself with our Golden Girls trivia to find out.

1 Who was the oldest Golden Girl in real life?

2 What is Dorothy's occupation?

3 What is Rose's maiden name?

4 How many Emmy awards did *The Golden Girls* win in total?

5 Which organ did Blanche offer to donate to her sister?

6 What was the name of the house chef who appeared in the pilot episode?

7 Which Golden Girl referred to her youthful self as 'a tall voluptuous blonde with a butt like granite'?

8 Which singer–songwriter starred as a girl scout called Daisy who held Rose's teddy bear to ransom with a toy gun?

9 Who played the man that Dorothy marries at the end of the series?

10 What is the name of Dorothy's brother, who Sophia continually refers to in a less-than-favourable manner?

11 Name the singing duo that Dorothy and Sophia dressed up as for Halloween in season five.

12 Which Golden Girl has a father called 'Big Daddy'?

13 In season one, which animal were the Golden Girls breeding in their garage to make money on the fur trade?

14 Which Golden Girl originally went for the role of Blanche, only to play another character?

15 What was the name of Sophia's husband and Dorothy's father?

16 How many episodes of *The Golden Girls* were originally broadcast?
a 110   b 160   c 180

17 Dorothy's son is caught in bed with the daughter of which Golden Girl?

18 Who was the tallest baby in Brooklyn and had a rash on her face for the first two years of her life?

19 Which Golden Girl has a brother who comes to Miami to announce his commitment ceremony with another man?

20 The girls are arrested on the way to a movie premiere under the suspicion of being prostitutes. Who was the star of this film?

You can never be over-dressed or over-educated.

ANSWERS: 1. Betty White 2. teacher 3. Lindström 4. eleven 5. kidney 6. Coco 7. Sophia 8. Jenny Lewis 9. Leslie Nielsen 10. Phillip 11. Sonny and Cher 12. Blanche 13. mink 14. Rose 15. Salvadore 16. 180 episodes 17. Rose 18. Dorothy 19. Blanche 20. Burt Reynolds

90

What kind of FRIEND ARE YOU?

0–5: *Golden Girls* n00b

You only remember a few sketchy details about *The Golden Girls* from when you watched it with grandma in the eighties. You need to watch all seven seasons immediately!

6–10: *Golden Girls* enthusiast

You've seen some episodes recently and enjoyed them, but you haven't given it the full sixty-nine hour rewatch. Make some popcorn and get to it!

11–15: *Golden Girls* super-fan

You are all over the finer details of the show and consider yourself something of an aficionado. Just one more casual pass of the entire series and you may reach expert level!

16–20: *Golden Girls* expert

Were you an original cast member of *The Golden Girls*? You could find your way around the Golden Girls' house blind-folded and in the dark.

The opening bars of *The Golden Girls* theme song are instantly familiar to anyone who watched TV in the eighties and nineties.

Thank You for Being a Friend, the ICONIC THEME TUNE

The theme is based on the original 1978 song 'Thank You for Being a Friend', written and performed by singer–songwriter Andrew Gold. This was one of Gold's most successful songs – his song 'Lonely Boy' gave him his biggest hit in 1977 when it reached the US top ten. Gold famously claimed that despite the song's popularity, 'Thank You for Being a Friend' only took him 'about an hour' to write (I bet the royalty cheques make him glad he did).

The song was shortened and re-recorded by Cynthia Fee to serve as the theme song to both *The Golden Girls* and *Golden Palace*. Other than being a catchy tune, the lyrics seemed to truly define the relationship between the Golden Girls.

The popularity of *The Golden Girls* resulted in the song being adapted for many television and radio advertisements after the series ended. It is a challenge to think of a more iconic television theme song. For many, hearing it decades after the final episode aired still conjures up enough nostalgia to prevent just about anyone from changing the channel.

THE LEGACY OF THE GOLDEN GIRLS

Looking back now, it is hard to quantify the impact that *The Golden Girls* has had on popular culture. Since it first graced our screens 1985, audiences have adored the four sassy, hilarious women and the television landscape was changed forever.

Thanks to a variety of storylines mixing the everyday with the provocative, *The Golden Girls* has the rare honour of being beloved by both mainstream audiences and a diverse range of communities around the world. Never a show to shy away from the big issues, controversial topics were craftily packaged into an easy-to-digest half hour that informed as well as entertained. Some taboo topics were deadly serious, others were just dead funny – who could forget the hilarious scene when the girls bought condoms before heading off to the Bahamas?

The Golden Girls also had a strong feminist message woven into the very fabric of the show. What isn't feminist about four women making a life for themselves without the presence or approval of men? Each Golden Girl lived a full social life, and everyone but Sophia held down a job. Yes, there were plenty of eligible bachelors, dates and even engagements, but the themes of female independence and friendship prevailed in each episode.

More than thirty years later and the legacy of *The Golden Girls* still resonates within the television industry. *The Golden Girls* paved the way for all-women prime-time comedy casts, precipitating sitcoms like *Designing Women*, *Living Single* and *Desperate Housewives*. Just consider which *Sex and the City* character aligns to which Golden Girl and contemplate the far-reaching influence of the show.

The Golden Girls may have made us laugh while teaching us a thing or two, but most importantly, the Girls taught us the importance of friendship above all else.

To Rue, Bea, Betty and Estelle – thank you for bringing us *The Golden Girls*. To Blanche, Dorothy, Rose and Sophia – thank you for being a friend.

Smith Street Books

Published in 2017 by Smith Street Books
Melbourne | Australia
smithstreetbooks.com

ISBN: 978-1-925418-56-9

CIP data is available from the National Library of Australia.

Publisher: Paul McNally
Project editor: Hannah Koelmeyer
Author: Emma Lewis
Design: Kate Barraclough
Illustration: Chantel de Sousa, The Illustration Room

Printed & bound in China by C&C Offset Printing Co., Ltd.

Book 42
10 9 8 7 6 5

Please note: This book is in no way affiliated
with the creators or copyright holders of
The Golden Girls. We're just really big fans.
Please don't sue us.